I0413467

Communism & Islamism
How Communism enabled the coming Islamic invasion &
destruction of Western Civilization
by
Mark N. Alexander

This book is dedicated to all those who fought and paid with their blood to preserve our culture & civilization throughout the ages. This book is dedicated to Western Civilization.

Table of Contents

Prologue

"Until now, the world we've known has been a world divided, a world of barbed wire and concrete blocks, conflict and cold war. Now, we can see a new world coming into view. A world in which there is the very real prospect of a new world order. In the words of Winston Churchill, a "world order" in which "the principles of justice and fair play ... protect the weak against the strong ..." A world where the United Nations, freed from cold war stalemate, is poised to fulfill the historic vision of its founders. A world in which freedom and respect for human rights find a home among all nations."

-President George Bush Sr.

With the end of the cold war, it seemed that there would finally be an everlasting peace. President George Bush Senior in his famous speech after the fall of communist Russia, spoke of a new world order. In the President's speech, he spoke of a world that was united under the rule of law, under a new system, guided by the principles of the United Nations. No longer would there be a divide between nations of North or South, East or West; humanism would be the creed of the new age. Democracy and Capitalism would be the guide to a globalized, secular westernized vision for the world. A new civil religion in which all humanity will prostrate in atonement for past economic sin. The West has won, and it is their system that will rule the rest of the world. Just as peace was achieved between the West and the communist East, accordingly the rest of the world would follow per the democratic peace theory. The West at that point was preparing to unarm and enjoy the fruits of economic prosperity without the fear of war. This utopic vision of harmony between all the sons of Adam did not last very long, the never ending peace was soon tested by an old foe of Christendom, a foe with origins from Arabia, with a new tactical weapon, the weapon of terrorism. Christendom had much experience with this long forgotten foe, after all, it had been at war with Islam since the Islamic conquest of Byzantium territory in the late 7th century AD. Forgotten perhaps because the evolution of politics caused historical amnesia. Christendom finally defeated the Islamic enemy, when the Turks, a last futile attempt to save their ever weakening empire, sided with Germany during WWI. With the defeat of the axis powers, the Caliphate was no more; the last Islamic empire had fallen, the Ottoman Empire was finished, and many Muslims at the time feared Islam as a religion would soon follow into the grave of history. With the collapse of the Caliphate, Turkey Westernized and became a secular state under Mostafa Kamal Atatürk , the rest of the Ottoman empire fell was divided amongst Western powers and fell to

Western Colonialism. Islam as a serious foe had suffered a dismantling blow. Islamic nations adapted Protestant Christian principles founded during the enlightenment period. Most of the Ottoman territory now controlled by Western powers with the installation of puppet Kings. With Western liberal ideals and philosophies being taught at many of the newly resurrected universities across the Muslim world, progressive movements dissolved Sharia Islamic laws replaced by English Common Law, and the Napoleonic Code. In a matter of two generations from the desolation of the Ottoman Empire, the entire Muslim world was secularized and effectively made European. No other time since the Islamic invasion of North Africa in the late 7th century did North Africa look and feel like it naturally would have if Islam had never advanced and conquered it. North Africa prospered in many ways, winning the rights of women, minorities, and the poor. The protestant Christian ideals founded by enlightenment period Christian thinkers were now the laws of the land of most North African ex-Ottoman Muslim states. Dr. Alvin J. Schmidt notes in his book *How Christianity Changed the World; h*ow the origins of Western economics and laws are institutions attributed to and founded on Christian principles.[i] During the same period, new ideas to counteract Capitalism, and Christianity had been fostering for half a century; the political philosophies of Fascism, Socialism, Communism and Islamism. Through these different philosophies, Christendom would be transformed from the inside out, not only changing world history, but setting up the ex-Christian nations of Europe and America, now known as simply the *West*, for self destruction. According to my calculations, by the middle of our current century, Europe will be inflamed in a bloody civil war, a war of survival, a war for the livelihood of Western civilization. The root cause of this destruction has everything to do with an unlikely alliance of two philosophies whom don't share the same ideology, but have an important common enemy that has been like a lump in the throat for both, that enemy is Christianity and its powerful civilization found in the West. The enemies of Western Christian civilization had been perceived as long defeated, but they are still with us, and one philosophy will help the other destroy the *West*. The two philosophies are Communism & Islamism. Communism sees religion in general and Christianity in particular as the main obstacle for the peasantry and working class. The class struggle in Marxist/Lenin view is retained due to Christianity. To Marxist/ Leninists, "Religion teaches those who toil in poverty all their lives to be resigned and patient in this world, and consoles them with the hope of reward in heaven. As for those who live upon the labor of others, religion teaches them to be "charitable" thus providing a justification for exploitation and, as it were, also a cheap ticket to heaven likewise. "Religion is the opium of the people." Religion is a kind of spiritual intoxicant, in which the slaves of capital drown their humanity, and blunt their desire for a decent human existence."[ii] For Marx & Lenin, the only way humanity can reach and evolve to a state of utopia was the end of all religions in particularly Christianity. Christianity was the main target since Marx & Lenin lived within the borders of Christendom. Another reason their focus on Christianity was Christianity's close relationship to capitalism. Capitalism and the idea of maximizing profits drove the advent of colonialism and the slave trade, both are a dark glooming cloud over Christendom's history. Communists focused on the existing ideas that had already emerged at the time of Marx, the idea of the separation of church and state. Communists sought to reinterpret the separation of church and state, successfully so, over time, challenging the understanding of the traditional interpretation of separation of church and state as philosophized by Protestant Christian thinkers such as Martin Luther, Calvin and others in which Western civilization had adopted. The atheistic propaganda allowed to circulate in the public square in the West was due to the evolution of Christian principles which led to freedom of expression which the communist's used to their advantage, spreading their ideas like a atheistic virus across the West, infecting Western civilization which eventually caused the moral decay of society, from a Christian perspective, but also the endangerment of Western civilization to the rising power of Fascistic Islamism, which threatens the very existence of Western civilization. Somehow, Islam recovered and is back with a vengeance, back on the old trail of world domination and subjugation under the law of Allah,[iii] [1] under the banner of Islamic Law also known as the Sharia, الشريعة السلامية or Sharia law. Although the old foe is not as strong as it was once upon a time during its early years of conquests deep into Byzantium, yet there is something interesting one must consider, Christendom is no longer morally strong as it once was as well, the will to fight in the name of Christ to protect other Christians or to stop the advance of Islam is not something modern day Westerners are ready to shoulder, although they have the military and economic means to win easily. Militarily, with the United States leading the West, the West has no match. The West is also technologically superior to all other civilizations. Economically, the West is also superior, despite the black gold of which much belongs by and large to the Muslim world. The West is lacking foresight. They lack heart, they lack the will to fight. The will to fight had given way to the philosophies of the new age mainly by the ingrained ideas of atheism by Marx, Engels, Lenin and other comrades. Although the West is led by the United States, the United States does not make all the decisions on behalf of Western Civilization. Europe has been under the sway of Marxism indiscreetly for a long time. This was best witnessed after the Islamic terrorist attacks on the Madrid train system in which the Spaniards blamed themselves for the attacks, justifying the cause and blaming their government that had sent a meager 1300 troops to aid the coalition in the Iraq war. Instead of the Spaniards seeking revenge for the cowardly terrorist acts that took the lives of 191 Spanish citizens and wounded 1800 others, they appeased the Islamists, and the new liberal leftist government withdrew Spanish troops in utter defeat. They simply have been taught from birth to self loath through their corrupted Marxist/Leninist view of Christian/ Capitalist history taught by communist leaning educators under the disguise of liberal progressives. Warriors of the past who had a strong Christian conviction in fighting a moral and justified war according to the *Just War Theory* as taught by St. Augustine and St. Thomas Aquinas, fought with their hearts, to preserve their civilization and their culture which was rooted in Christianity; unity and faith were their strengths, and the promise of an afterlife to those who died for Christ.[iv] The war against Islamism lacks this type of heart. Western nations are not united, the people are divided along conservative/liberal lines. With the number of Church attendance at an all time low. The lack of belief in an afterlife will continue to cause appeasement after appeasement, till Europeans become minorities in their own country. Besides, even communists were willing to die for their own cause but to fight for European or Western civilization viewed from the Marxist/ Leninist philosophy, is an actual attempt to reintroduce a neo colonial agenda by the capitalists in which they hope to subjugated poorer peoples of weaker nations into a new modern day slave like exploitation. Communism fervently believes in the idea of humanism, in that eventually we will all be one in communism. Roughly 46% of former Christendom, the EU, are atheist or agnostic[v] while 51% of those that believed in "a God" the majority of that group no longer believe in organized religion, or in Christianity.[vi] With the large numbers of Muslims now living in Europe, the poll does not distinguish which God from the 51% did Europeans believe in. So how many Christians or native Europeans still believe in the Christian God? It varies by country, but in general the number is at a low 30%. Islamists are Jihadists, they are fighting a holy war that they perceive is ordered by Allah (God). That war has historically been by and large against Christianity and its civilization. We know that Westerners fought throughout history to preserve Christianity and Western civilization from Islam. Will they be willing to do the same today for a Western civilization that is rooted in Atheism? Essentially fight for the idea of preserving the freedom to believe in absolutely nothing. Will Westerners die for atheism instead of living under a fascistic Islamist system? Or will they continue to appease Islamist's in the hope that we all can coexist in the attempt to hopefully over time turn Muslims into atheists as well, and then we could all live peacefully. Only time can answer the mystery of these questions, however, according to statistics, while Europeans are quickly losing faith in any god, Muslims are becoming more Muslim, meaning more fundamental, each new decade. The evidence is overwhelming, and the reasons for this goes beyond the scope of this small book, but a good example can be seen in pictures from the 1920s to the 1970s in which pictures from that time speak a thousand words. Look at pictures of Egypt, Syria, Palestine, Libya, Morocco, Jordan or any other Arab/ Muslim majority country from that period and compare the landscape to today, you will see that back then those countries, the people, looked, dressed and acted like Westerners or un-Islamic. Today, the overwhelming veiling of women is a testament to the re-Islamization of the Middle East. [2]

Cairo University Class of 1978

Cairo University Class of 2004

Egyptian Beach 1950s

Egyptian Beach 2008

Chapter 1

Lenin's Philosophy (Anti-religious/Anti-capitalist)

Religion is a kind of spiritual intoxicant, in which the slaves of capital drown their humanity, and blunt their desire for a decent human existence.

- Lenin

Lenin's Philosophy like that of Marx and Engels was that of materialism. Although all three were Atheists, they often identified themselves with materialism because it sounded less interstice to a Christian believer of whom they looked to propagate into the social workers/communist movement. "Materialism means any theory that considers the facts of the universe to be sufficiently explained by the existence of nature and matter. For the materialist, the human mind is considered a product of the development of matter and its movement, with no reference to soul or spirit. For economic materialists the substructure of material relationships determines the superstructure of societal values including religious superstitions."[vii] For Marx and Lenin, materialism was an absolute truth. The communist theory was established around the notion that capitalism exploited workers for the gains of the capitalist or the bourgeois. Their war against religion and Christianity in particular, not only stemmed from their atheistic beliefs, but also on the premise that Christianity supported this economic capitalist structure. Lenin taught that "religion teaches those who toil in poverty all their lives to be resigned and patient in this world, and consoles them with the hope of reward in heaven. As for those who live upon the labor of others, religion teaches them to be "charitable" thus providing a justification for exploitation and, as it were, also a cheap ticket to heaven likewise. Religion is the opium of the people."[viii] Whether through his own conviction or belief, Lenin knew that for communism to succeed, religion needed to be eradicated. Once people were off the "opium of the masses" to use his words, socialism would naturally be installed by the proletariat leading eventually to communism. This of course would be no easy task. The Russian Orthodox Church was a powerful institution in Tsarist Russia. The Russian government subsidized the Church, in return; the Church officially backed the government, endorsing its policies. At the time of the Russian revolution of 1917; 85 percent of rural peasants were illiterate, and 70 percent of the entire Russian population was also illiterate.[ix] To Lenin, this helped the Church preserve a hold on the masses due to their illiteracy. The illiteracy that he holds the Church responsible for, naturally help Lenin in his own attempts at controlling the masses and in inciting them to raise a communist revolution with doses of communist ideology opium for the masses, replacing Christ with himself as the iconic image of worship. Not only were many of these Christians of Russia superstitious, adapting pre-Christian era mythology within their worship, but they also hardly had any real conviction in Christianity, at least deep enough in faith and knowledge to obstruct Lenin's views and defend Christianity from the mounting evidence Lenin provided from the sciences through evidence and rationalism. Around 1905 Constantine Pobedonostsev, chief procurator of the Orthodox Church, described with a clear conscience what he considered the religious mentality of the peasantry at the time.

> Our clergy teaches little and seldom. The Bible does not exist for the illiterate people... In far off parts of the country the people understand absolutely nothing as to the meaning of the words of the service, not even the Lord's Prayer, which is often repeated with alterations which altogether destroy its meaning. And yet, in all those primitive minds there is erected, as in ancient Athens, an altar to the unknown God, and they resign their lives to Providence.[x]

Lenin faced a tactical dilemma. Should the proletariat adopt atheism as a necessary prerequisite to the workers revolution or should the revolution come first? To Marx and Lenin, Atheism was a necessity for a successful transformation of society, without Atheism, that society could never reach its ultimate highest degree of potential. According to Marx and Lenin, religion sits at the opposite end of the spectrum by stifling a society from their highest degree of potential by replacing works to make a utopic society on earth for works that a factitious god would merit to the believer, awarding him with a utopic paradise in the afterlife. Lenin looked to Marx's writings for the answer. The young Marx worried that the Christian peasantry and factory worker were so immersed in the idea that a Christian must obey the ruler that God had placed on the throne and adhere to the mother Church, to the extent that a revolution would never muster enough courage by a mass uprising of the majority, there simply wouldn't be one. The young Marx therefore sought that atheism should be a prerequisite to the communist revolution. As Marx matured, his ideas changed in the opposite direction, believing that if the revolution happened first, this would bring about the death of God and religion. The Old Bolshevik, Nikolai Bukharin said it best, "the transition from the society that makes an end of capitalism to the society that is completely free from all traces of class division and class struggle will bring about the natural death of all religion and all superstition."[xi] Marx had a plan that would work perfectly if done properly. It focused on eliminating the roots of the social culture through economics that which Christianity was built upon and had thrived. When these roots or conditions were changed, religion would wither away and the transformation of society would result. Lenin was convinced of Marx's plan on how a minority like Lenin's Bolsheviks could convince the majority of the Christian peasantry and workers to join his labor revolution. After which, when people reached the utopic state of earthly paradise due to their own merits, instead of waiting on God to change their condition, man essentially would become his own god and his own savior. With the contribution of materialism, man would build his own society without the obstruction of religion on his freedom, he would be morally free of immorality, he would be rehabilitated off the Church induced opium, therefore; there would no longer be a need for religion, religion would eventually die or at least the few adherents left would be a minority practicing in privacy and quietly. Convinced of this, Lenin decided to worry about Christianity later. Lenin even encouraged Christian workers to join the ranks of the Russian Social Democratic Labor Party. He also quickly authorized their induction into educating them on the principles of Marxism through propaganda without seriously offending their religious beliefs. "Still years from power, Lenin concentrated on practical ways of combating religious belief through the development of class-consciousness and "patiently preaching proletarian solidarity and the scientific world outlook." He persuaded his followers that knowing how to combat religion meant explaining to the masses the source of faith in a materialist way."[xii] Lenin's task at first was to create an army of dissenters whom no longer took orders from the Church. A force that would demand their rights of higher wages and shorter work hours. He needed a force that had converted to his beliefs that God was created in man's image, because man needed a god to place their worries upon, out of their own short comings. He needed fellow atheists.

> Fear made the gods. Fear of the blind force of capital, blind because it cannot be foreseen by the masses of the people, a force which at every step in the life of the proletarian and small proprietor threatens to inflict, and does inflict, sudden, unexpected, accidental ruin, destruction, pauperism, prostitution, death from starvation. Such is the root of modern religion. - Lenin

1950s communist feminism propaganda flyer

Chapter 2

Lenin's Terror Tactics : *a war against God & Country*

All into the churches! ... by all that is permitted by Christian conscience, we can and are obliged to fight for faith and church, for the trampled treasures of our soul.... Let them cross our dead bodies. Let them shoot us, shoot innocent children and women. Let us go with crosses, ikons, unarmed, with prayers and hymns, let Cain and Judas kill us! The time has come to go to martyrdom and suffering!"

- Russian Orthodox Patriarch Tikhon

-

A chain of events occurred that brought forth the Bolshevik revolution. Just like today with the Islamist groups, many have the same end goal but differ on how to achieve that goal. Some groups are more extreme than others in their approach in politics and tactics. Once upon a time, it all started with one group and one idea, eventually members of the group differed in opinion and split the group by forming their own group, etc. The same can be said for the communist revolution in Russia. The Socialists were a group of men who professed to speak on behalf of the working class, the vanguard of the proletariat. The workers by in large were Christians not atheists, and their demands were pathetically ambitious when crossed with the Marxist dream of socialist Utopia. Their demands were simple, better wages, shorter working hours, and better working conditions. To the socialists, these illiterate people could never achieve Utopia of a classless society without the help of the vanguard. A conflict arose between the socialists in 1903 that split the group into two, the Bolsheviks (under Lenin) and the Mensheviks.

Bolshevik translates as the majority faction, the Mensheviks being the minority; confusingly, the Mensheviks were the majority faction until 1917. Both factions agreed that the three-century-old Romanov dynasty had to go, but whereas Lenin and the Bolsheviks advocated a core of professional revolutionaries under centralized leadership who would lead workers into revolution, the Mensheviks proposed a more gradual approach. Come the revolution, the Bolsheviks would immediately transfer power to the urban working classes, the dictatorship of the proletariat. The Mensheviks followed the more traditional Marxist thinking that Russia had first to develop as a capitalist economy before being ready to undergo a transition to socialism.[xiii]

The Bolsheviks under the leadership of Lenin were not willing to compromise and wait an endless amount of years to achieve the classless dream. The Mensheviks staged protests, many of which were crushed by the governments powerful hand. The more oppression posed by the Tsarist government, the more resentment from the workers and peasants accumulated, making the socialist case more legitimate. The situation around the world also aided in the bringing about of the Communist revolution in Russia. "On 28 June 1914, the heir to the Austrian-Hungarian throne, Franz Ferdinand, together with his wife, was assassinated in Sarajevo, capital of Bosnia. The Serbian perpetrators were members of a Bosnian-Serbian terrorist group, the Black Hand, who sought by violent means Serbia's independence from the Austrian-Hungarian Empire. The Serbian government had no hand in the assassination but it was to them that the Austrian– Hungarian government turned its anger, issuing Serbia an ultimatum designed to humiliate. The Serbians, unable to comply with the demands, found themselves at war with their powerful neighbor, who, as insurance, had sought the endorsement of the even more powerful Germany. It was to Russia, protector of all Slavs, that Serbia turned. The Tsar ordered the mobilization of his nation's military in order to wage war on Austria–

Hungary. He hoped, nonetheless, to avoid war with Germany. Germany, in turn, gave Russia twelve hours to halt its mobilization. The deadline passed, and on 1 August 1914, Germany declared war on Russia and, two days later, on France. The Great War had begun. Russia's war effort would draw in over fifteen million of its men; eight million soldiers or civilians were killed or wounded; and almost seventy million Russians living in the west of the empire found themselves at some point under enemy occupation."[xiv] Patriotism initially was high amongst the soldiers on the front, but quickly as Russia was dealt major military defeats, discontent with the war and rumors of treachery were spreading everywhere. In fact the Tsar was so furious, he fired the commander of the armed forces and led the campaign himself. The Germans had a tool they were ready to use, Lenin. Lenin at the time was living in exile in Geneva. The Germans knowing his anti-nationalism/ anti-Tsar stance and his view on the worldwide workers revolution worked in their favor. They offered him safe passage to Petrograd, which is St. Petersburg, where a workers strike was already in effect. They hoped that Lenin's presence would spark a revolution in which would weaken the Russian state into a peace agreement. The Germans themselves viewed Lenin with such fear, that they put him on a train with his room bolted shut, so that he did not infect the rest of the German riders on the train with his philosophy. Not long after Lenin arrived in Petrograd, the revolution had reached other cities and the Tsar abdicated his thrown. The Romanov dynasty was no more, a provisional socialist government was formed.

Chapter 3

The Bolsheviks Revolution : *A Minority becomes a Majority*

He who would learn to fly one day must first learn to stand and walk and run and climb and dance; one cannot fly into flying.

-Friedrich Nietzsche

By November 1917, the provisional government was made up mostly of Mensheviks whom quickly went from being the majority to a minority. The Mensheviks were not in any hurry to transform the society into a socialist one. For the time being, the Mensheviks sought a Russia that would follow Marx's theory that a nation cannot skip being capitalist before it evolved into socialism. Nonetheless, the Mensheviks one must always remember were communists at heart, their end goals of a classless, genderless, atheist utopia were the same as Lenin's Bolsheviks, they just differed on which road they should take at the fork. The laws enacted by the provisional government made some major breakthroughs in reform, freedom of expression was the most noted. The provisional government was at first endorsed by the Church however, the Church quickly realized that the new government had an atheistic agenda and soon thereafter the Church under its newly elected patriarch Tikhon would wage war on the new government. The Bolsheviks revolution then went underway. The Bolsheviks became the majority and went on the offensive creating the Red Guards under the non-partisan slogan, "power to the Soviets." The Bolsheviks, seized control of various government facilities including the Winter Palace, (the seat of the government) and points of communication. The Winter palace was easy to take, the Red Guard Subdued the Cossack guards, and women from the Women's Death Battalion. "The revolutionaries found Kerensky's cabinet and arrested them on the spot... meanwhile, Lenin, never one to expose himself to danger, donned his disguise, hid, and waited for news. In the end, the toppling of Kerensky's Provisional Government had been relatively bloodless and easy. There were no demonstrations, no violence."[xv] Lenin quickly went to work, the congress met and Lenin had no intentions of sharing the government with anyone but his Bolsheviks, even other socialist parties. Lenin going on his own principles and not that of Marx opened the meeting declaring a Socialist order. He then announced his *Decree on Peace,* proposing an immediate withdrawal of Russia from the great war. Lenin's second Decree was the Nationalization of all private property. Imagine on any given day the government coming to your house and declaring it for the people. Dividing your property among other people to come and live with you in your own home, that is what happened in Russia. The Church was one of the major points of attack by Lenin, nationalization of all private property also meant that the state now owned the Church and its billions of dollars in property. The nationalization read in part like this, "the monastic and church lands, with all their livestock, implements, farm buildings, and everything pertaining thereto, shall be placed under the control of the village land committees and the district Soviets of Peasants' Deputies, pending the meeting of the Constituent Assembly."[xvi] Lenin was moving to raise the rhetoric of terror against the Church by issuing a statement in a letter given to Soviets to hand over to the priests of local churches. If anyone was against the Bolshevik revolution they would be automatically condemned to death.

> If you are sincere, you must stand for a complete separation of the church from the state, for a separation of the school from the church, and insist that religion be regarded entirely and unconditionally as a private matter. If you do not accept these consistent demands of liberty, it means you are still a slave to inquisitorial traditions. It means that you are still hankering after government posts and the revenues attached to them, it means that you do not believe in the spiritual force of your weapon and that you still wish to take bribes from the government. If this is so, the class-conscious Russian workers will declare ruthless war on you.

-Lenin : Letter to the Church

Lenin knew that the Western idea of separation of Church and state would not be enough for his vision of Utopia. The separation for Lenin meant that the Church had no ties to the government, but the government still meddled in Church affairs. A good example in the modern scene is President Obama pushing Catholic institutions to cover birth control for its employees even though this goes against Catholic religious teaching. This is government not separating itself from religion. Trotsky summarized it best, he said "the separation of the church from the state, which we have established once and for all, by no means signifies that the state is indifferent to what is happening in the church."[xvii] The largest institution that clearly supported the Tsar and the Capitalist system was the Russian Orthodox Church. The Church became the main target for the Bolsheviks who knew its desolation would be a prerequisite to a successful socialist revolution. So, on the second day of power, as mentioned before, Lenin authorized the nationalization of all private property. What did this mean exactly? How would the atheist Bolsheviks, who were powerful, because they had the guns, yet still numbered in a minority when compared to the overall Christian population of 70 percent of Russians control the masses? which tactic would they use to instill fear in the Majority? Terrorism was the tactic of choice, in that it would provoke and terrorize the population into submission. But this came later, after other methods were not useful.

Chapter 4

The First Battle - *Soviet social engineers vs. the Church*

Lenin first ordered religious schools, including Orthodox seminaries, turned over to the Commissariat of Education. Second, Lenin ordered divorce laws to be secularized and births out of wedlock lawful. Third, Lenin required the civil registration of birth, marriage, and deaths and soon thereafter mandated that hundreds of years of past church records be turned over to the state.[xviii] A few weeks later it was time for the Soviets to test the waters even further by sending out the Red Guard to confiscate a very symbolic Church. If the Soviets could be successful in implementing their nationalization of Church property, then the Utopic vision would be within arm's length. Commissar of Welfare dispatched a squad of Kronstadt sailors. (The sailors were considered the most elite and best trained soldiers of Russia) They were dispatched to "St. Alexander Nevsky Monastery in Petrograd. The medieval hero Prince Alexander Nevsky was buried there, and it had become a symbol of the old order that the Bolsheviks were in a hurry to replace; Kollontai intended to convert the building into a rest home for war invalids."[xix] Upon arrival of the sailors, the church rang their bells in a frantic drastic cry for help, as was the tradition. The people of the village quickly dispersed to aid the Church. One of the priests was shot dead and the troops quickly retreated. The official Soviet paper quickly spinned the events, concluding that the Church was hostile to the troops by ringing their bells which according to the paper was meant for inciting the crowds to become violent against the government troops. Lenin realized the dangers of attacking the Church as the people were still by in large fearless and willing to die for Christ and "His Church." A new set of anti Christian laws were to be passed. Even if the laws couldn't be enacted at the time, they would eventually. A new decree passed by Lenin terminated any financial support for the clergy and for the up keeping of church buildings. Without the government funds, the church had no way of staying afloat.

Separation : *School & Church*

The future of any nation lies upon its youth. The next generation of Russians to Lenin had to be separated from the Church. The removal of God from the school curriculum was top priority.

> Thanks to the union of school and church, our young people were from their earliest years thralls to religious superstition, thus making it practically impossible to convey to their minds any integral outlook upon the universe. To one and the same question (for instance concerning the origin of the world) religion and science give conflicting answers, so that the impressionable mind of the pupil becomes a battleground between exact knowledge and the gross errors of obscurantist.[xx]

When the Bolsheviks took over the educational system at the end of 1917, they had the important task of converting 40,000 church schools into secular public schools that advocated to the children the beliefs of the new civil religion of Lenin. At that time there were 5 million students. Although most of the teachers were willing to teach their students in a non-religious manor they were not however willing to teach them atheism or materialism.

> In [the Bolshevik] method of attack they proceed on the theory that religion is not the result of an inborn force or impulse, but of training, of something that is superimposed from without. If children, they declare, are reared without religious guidance, they will grow up to be nonreligious, and then religion will dry up at the source and will die of its own accord[xxi]

It would take years before the Soviets could officially implement a truly secular, atheistic curriculum for school children. One must note that for Russia there was incredible advancements through the new secular school curriculum which was saturated with math and sciences. This attack on the authority of the Church in actuality helped the Church because the overall illiteracy in Russia dropped and with it the Church lost many of its non-biblical superstitions. Although many did lose their faith in Christ and the Church, the ones that remained faithful were able to modernize the Church, without losing its Orthodox traditions. An example of such superstition was the belief that when it rained, the rain was created by the Prophet Elijah.

Although the policy of the Soviets created generations of non-believers without any sense of Christian morality, it strengthened the Church in creating for it a push to modernize, perhaps making it more true to Christian principles of Christ and His apostles. Yet, all this was achieved through acts of State Terrorism which one can never agree that the ends justifies the means.

One must remember that Russia never had an enlightenment period like much of Western Europe in which over centuries ideas through Rationalism revolutionized the Catholic Church and its hold on State politics. The Russian Orthodox Church and Russia skipped 500 years of political evolution, they effectively went from the Dark Ages to the Jazz Age[1] of the 1920s in a flash instant.

---

[1] *The Jazz Age* relates to Jazz music which symbolically represents the changing cultural structure of the 1920s. Jazz is a lively and improvisational style of music which relates to the jazz age in which socially society became more lively itself. Jazz was introduced by African Americans which also suggests that the jazz age is a era of cultural acceptance.

Chapter 5

The Red Terror Campaign

"Everywhere in Petrograd and even in the most remote back streets printed proclamations appeared in which Soviet power was cursed and which called for bringing down God's anger on the heads of "atheists and terrorists."

Lenin soon realized that only through intimidation and terrorism could the voices opposing the revolution be stifled. He looked upon one man to carry this great responsibility upon his shoulders, Felix Dzerzhinsky. Lenin established a state terrorist organization known as the Cheka. The Cheka became the most feared government institution. It was established to combat counter revolutionary movements and sabotage. It was an instrument of terror, arresting and torturing members of other parties and anyone it deemed anti-Bolshevik without trial. Lenin said, "you cannot make a revolution wearing white gloves," to Lenin this was meant to be a short term method of eliminating revolutionary elements or scaring the rest through tactical terrorism into submission. To Lenin the ends justified the means in which the "ultimate goal of socialism was communism and with communism, the 'state would wither away,' to use Karl Marx's phrase. There would be no need for the mechanics of State control, and repression would become a memory of the past, and the 'entire society will be one office and one factory with equality of labor and equality of pay."[xxii] The dream was cut short with mass insurrections and protests due to a botched attempt at Democracy, a huge loss of Russian land that was vital to Russia's economy to the Germans during Lenin's peace proposal, and the attack on the Church and its institutions, left Russia in a Civil War. With the White Army fighting for God and Tsar, marching along in hope of recapturing the country, Lenin now had the license to terrorize. Lenin issued his famous decree on Red Terror:

> At this moment it is absolutely vital that the Chekas be reinforced.... to protect the Soviet Republic from its class enemies, who must all be locked up in concentration camps. Anyone found to have had any dealings with the White Guard organizations, plots, insurrections or riots will be summarily executed, and the names of all these people together with the reasons for their execution, will be announced publicly.[xxiii]

In a well regarded workers newspaper *Pravda* an article declared to the workers that "the time has come for us to crush the bourgeoisie or be crushed by it. The corruption of the bourgeoisie must be cleansed from our towns immediately. Files will now be kept on all men concerned, and those who represent a danger to the revolutionary cause will be executed... the anthem of the working class will be a song of hatred and revenge!"[xxiv] From their field offices the Cheka agents were sent out into the street to terrorize the citizens into submission to the Bolsheviks revolution. The Cheka's were ordered not to look for evidence as proof that the accused has acted or spoken against the Soviets but rather the Cheka was to ask anyone it doubted to which class he or she belonged, what their social origins were, and what education and profession they held. These questions would determine the fate of the accused. That is the true meaning of the Red terror.[xxv] The Cheka were so vicious that anyone could be accused as a counter revolutionary. From the accused were people conducting private businesses, drunkenness, and even being late for work as counter revolutionary.[xxvi] There were also many whom were falsely accused by their neighbors in hoping to get out of debt to them or because they simply didn't like them. The Cheka in two month executed 15,000 "counter revolutionaries." To put things into prospective, under the Tsar rule from 1825 to 1917, there were recorded 6,321 executions.[xxvii] Many were hung by the Cheka from street lights and left out to rot, the intention was to send a clear message to the rest of the population now living in terror, to submit to the Revolution or succumb to the same fate. With the defeat of the Whites, the Civil war had come to an end. By the end of the Civil war the Cheka had arrested and place over 70,000 counter revolutionaries in concentration camps. These camps were old monasteries that the Cheka forcefully took over from the Orthodox Church. "over 2.3 million acres of monastery and convent land had been handed over to the state in the name of Russia's peasantry. (Eventually all

10.8 million acres the monasteries had owned would be lost to them.) out of 1,025 monasteries existing before World War I, 673 had been dissolved. The state had stripped from the monasteries 1,112 leased houses, 708 hotels, 602 cattle sheds, 435 dairy farms, 311 beehives, 277 hospitals and asylums, and 84 factories. By 1923 there was very little left. Most monastic property either had been appropriated by peasants at the time of the Revolution or had been confiscated by the state during the following four years. Any land left to the monks was too remote to be of any use to the government. Although the land was gone, most of the buildings remained with somewhat altered functions. An Orthodox writer sent this report out of the country in early 1926: "Not all monasteries are closed. Here and there they still exist under the name of "laboring communities." Even in the capital they are still to be found. Of course the number of ikons has been very much reduced. Sometimes the monasteries have been transformed into colonies where aged cripples or invalids are allowed to pass the remainder of their lives in the guise of custodians and keepers of the sacred objects and relics that have been declared to be objects of art and worthy of being kept in museums."[xxviii]

New anti-Christian laws were passed during this time. If the Church and any of its members violated any of these laws they would be considered counter revolutionary, in which such treachery carried with it a death sentence. The Cheka under Lenin's ordered the targeting of Kulaks, who were considered class enemies because they had gotten rich off of other peasants. The Kulaks were peasants themselves, but they were more efficient peasants. Lenin declared war on them and encouraged other peasants to kill them. With this effective war on the Kulaks, the nation's food supply was halted and the country went into famine. "Lenin dispatched gangs of Red Guards into the villages to requisition grain from the peasants, peasants who had very little in the first place for the provision of the cities and its workers. Those that resisted the demands to hand over their stocks were either shot or deported."[xxix] Millions died in the famine. Socialism, was a system that was supposed to lift the working class from the bottomless pit of poverty to a state of equality with those who were of the higher class.

What socialism/communist brought on Russia and its satellite states over 70 years of communist rule was an attack on people's faiths, death, war, oppression, famine and hunger like no other political/economic system the world had ever experienced before. It brought about anarchy and lawlessness, unprecedented immorality, and a lack of freedoms. The argument is made that the true utopic society was never achieved in Communist Russia. Placing most of the blame on Western capitalist states, for bad leadership such as under the paranoid schizophrenic Stalin and other leaders.

The communist system eventually collapsed in Russia, but the ideas of socialism have encroached into the capitalist West, which over the years, created the welfare continent. Lenin's voice lives on; Leninism and Marxist philosophy are endangering the future of Western civilization leading into the 21st century. All that was accomplished in Russia in the early years of the Bolshevik revolution are already commonplace throughout Western Civilization, that is the separation of Church and School, the separation of Church and State, the genderless feminist society, the idea of materialism, immorality and atheism. Most of the ideas circulating as common Western values are stemmed from communist philosophy.

Chapter 6

Islamists & Communists : the axis of evil

"Mankind today is on the brink of a precipice. Humanity is threatened not only by nuclear annihilation but by the absence of values. The West has lost its vitality and Marxism has failed. At this crucial and bewildering juncture, the turn of Islam and the Muslim community has arrived."

-Sayyid Qutb

One might read the title to this chapter and wonder how could two polar end philosophies form a partnership or an alliance? After all, communists put much of the blame on religion, and Islam is not any less guilty in the eyes of communists than Christianity. In fact, Islam to the communist is a much harder force to reckon with because there is absolutely no separation of Mosque and state in Islam the way there is in Christianity. "Islam is not simply a religion, it is an entire sociopolitical economic system. Where in Christianity, one can argue, that Christ was for the separation of Church and State, referencing several gospel verses, famously Matthew 22:20, "render onto creasers which is creasers and unto God what is God's." The argument could be made for Christianity that man's own evils caused corruption in the Church that caused corruption in Christian economics. The same argument cannot be made for Islam. Islam's Sunni's have four different schools of thought. The Hanafi school, the Maliki, the Shafi'i and the Hanbali. Each school has presented an understanding of Islamic Law. All four schools agree on 75 percent of their legal conclusions.[xxx] The Shia have a similar understanding toward Islamic Law from their own schools of thought. Islamic Law, according to the Muslims, is divine law. The Islamists have a dedication to seeing this law applied to every nation on earth. Clearly, Islamic law is completely polar opposite to communism, yet they are in an alliance whether they know it or not. Both philosophies have helped the other gain ground in the West, where the other couldn't have done so without the other. There goals are different yet similar in that they both seek world domination through their own vision of a new world order. For the communists, it is summed up best in the last paragraph of the Communist Manifesto.

> In short, the Communists everywhere support every revolutionary movement
> against the existing social and political order of things. In all these movements
> they bring to the front, as the leading question in each, the property question,
> no matter what its degree of development at the time. Finally, they labor

everywhere for the union and agreement of the democratic parties of all countries. The Communists disdain to conceal their views and aims. They openly declare that their ends can be attained only by the forcible overthrow of all existing social conditions. Let the ruling classes tremble at a Communistic revolution. The proletarians have nothing to lose but their chains. They have a world to win. Working men of all countries, unite![xxxi]

For Islam,

In all these Islam saw one embracing unity which took in the universe, the soul, and all human life. Its aim was to unite earth and heaven in one world; to join the present world and the world to come in one faith; to link spirit and body in one humanity; correlate worship and work one life. It sought to bring all these into one path, the path which leads to Allah.[xxxii]

Sayyid Qutb published his book "Social Justice in Islam" in 1949. His book was written similar to that of the Communist Manifesto. Explaining the social order of the world in how he saw it, and asserts how Islam is the solution to the world's problems. He carefully articulates the errors found in Christianity and in communism according to his views, and makes the case for Islam. He argues that "Christianity looks at man only from the standpoint of his spiritual desires which seeks to crush down human instincts in order to encourage those desires."[xxxiii] Mainly a similar argument that Lenin made in which the Church encouraged people not to protest their miserable lives, because a Christian was essentially living for the world to come. According to Qutb, "Christ came only to preach spiritual purity, mercy, kindness, tolerance, chastity, and abstinence, and to moderate certain restrictions that had been imposed on the children of Israel or that they themselves had invented... he attached no importance to the narrow traditions of the priests and the scribes... Christ's concern was with the moral and the spiritual realm."[xxxiv] To Qutb, Christianity was missing something essential, because Christianity was essentially acetic. "By its nature... it is to despise the world, and to seek rather the Lords Kingdom in the heavenly world."[xxxv] For Qutb, Christianity only dealt with the spiritual, but left a vacuum in how the world should be governed.

As for communism, according to Qutb, it only deals with the social economic issues of mankind. It's focus is on equality of wages but leaves the person seeking spiritual desire. For Qutb, Islam unites the two, the spiritual and the worldly. For Qutb, Islam is the perfect medium between Christianity and communism. It fills the void of both philosophies.

> The Islamic faith provides equity and justice for society and establishes justice for the whole of the human sphere. It also frees Islam from the narrow interpretation of justice as understood by Communism. For, justice to the Communist is an equality of wages in order to prevent economic discrimination; but within recent days when the theory has come into opposition with practice, Communism has found itself unable to achieve this equality. Justice in Islam is in human equality, envisaging the adjustment of all values, of which the economic is but one. [xxxvi]

Like Communism, the only way for the world to achieve the "beauty of Islam" is for the entire world to submit itself to Allah and his Laws as brought by and through the actions of the Prophet Mohammad and his companions. The world should be given a chance to embrace Islam, if they choose to reject Islam, then the Muslim should embark on a Jihad and slaughter the enemies of Allah till every tongue professes that there is no God but Allah and his prophet is Mohammad. [xxxvii]

> Islam has the right to take the initiative. Islam is not a heritage of any particular race or country; this is God's religion and it is for the whole world. It has the right to destroy all obstacles in the form of institutions and traditions which limit man's freedom of choice... The reasons for Jihad... Is to establish God's authority on the earth; to arrange human affairs according to the true guidance provided by God; to abolish all the Satanic forces and Satanic systems of life; to end the Lordship of one man over others since all men are creatures of God and no one has the authority to make them his servants to make arbitrary laws for them...
>
> - Sayyid Qutb

Like Lenin, Qutb believed that the peace and utopia that their philosophies promised the world would only be achieved after forcefully eradicating all obstacles through violent coercion. The same obstacle that stood in the way of communism was and is the same obstacle that stood and stands in the way of Islam; that is Christianity. The enemy of Islam has traditionally been Christianity from the very beginnings of Islam. The entire known world, the inheritance of the Greeks, the Roman empire, the lands of antiquity all belonged to Byzantium. Islam was established in Arabia, right on the borders of the Byzantine Empire. If Islam was ever to rule the world, they had to rule from Europe. If Islam could depose of the most advanced society known to man, then surly it was from God. Their main obstacle was and is Christianity and its Civilization. Not so much on a philosophical level, but rather on an economic military level. Islam from the very beginning, from its inception, waged a war against the Christian civilization. Islam led a successful campaign over the centuries, gobbling up more than half the lands that made up Byzantium. In its height, the Muslim armies sacked Constantinople the Capital of Byzantium also known as the New Rome and changed its name to Istanbul. It was not until the late 18th century that Islam started weakening and was on a constant downward spiral. It succumbed finally to Western powers when the Ottomans were defeated by the Allies in WWI. The Ottoman Empire was defeated, the Caliphate was abolished, and most of its lands were now colonies of Western powers. Yet, there are Islamists whom dream of the return of this old glorious Islamic empire in which the Caliphate will rule the world under the command of God's Law the Islamic Sharia. The one true obstacle to this Islamist utopic world view is as was in the past, Christian Europe. While the Islamists like Qutb and others spoke and wrote and dreamt of an Islamic Empire that ruled the world, the other enemy of the West and Christianity was slowly weakening into the 1980s. United States President Ronald

Regan and Pope John Paul II worked together in bringing about the collapse of the Soviet Union.[xxxviii] How much influence John Paul had on the collapse of the Soviet Union is probably exaggerated, although he was for sure a defiant Crusader in Poland. The realities for the demise of communism in Russia were many, but one main point in its downfall was the successes of capitalism in achieving a society that was truly free, that had a much higher living standard for its citizens, more than that of any communist nation. Capitalist systems had created an increasingly wealthy middle-class unlike any socialist country could produce. The people in communist states were talking, and the old Lenin tactics of terrorism were no longer succeeding in breaking down the people into submission. Although communism failed in Russia, the communists that lived all over the world and for our purposes in the West continued in their objective as it has always been to slowly change the West from within. The dangerous communists that lived in the West were not the ones that tried to initiate Lenin's terror tactics, as those who tried failed miserably unlike Lenin who succeeded in Russia. The real danger to the West was from the hidden communists that posed as everyday people but were bent on changing the West and its economic social structures from within. These infiltrators concluded that Marx's early writings were correct, and that Lenin made a mistake by thinking that atheism would proceed after the communists took power, they were now asserting that atheism must take place first and then the world would move towards socialism and then eventually into communism. Internal sabotage and infiltration was the tactic of choice. Communists infiltrated the West, posing as anything but communist. They are now labeled as progressives or liberals, but in the mid 20th century were seen as ordinary everyday Westerners. They joined the ranks of professionals. These undercover communists became professors, lawyers, doctors, artists, judges, politicians, movie stars, etc... and through human contact and freedom in democracy, they would slowly change the West from within.

> ...the first step in the revolution by the working class, is to raise the proletariat to the position of ruling as to win the battle of democracy. The proletariat will use its political supremacy to wrest, by degrees, all capital from the bourgeoisie, to centralize all instruments of production in the hands of the State, i.e., of the proletariat organized as the ruling class; and to increase the total of productive forces as rapidly as possible. [xxxix]

These undercover communists mainly went underground due to Western governments attempts at combating communist terrorists. Many therefore went underground, hiding their true beliefs and intentions. Whether this was an established tactic or sheer luck, it has worked in that it has fundamentally changed the culture of Western civilization in many ways, for example the creation of the welfare state and the West's extreme attempts at secularization in opposition to religion, in particularly Christianity; which is the main obstacle to communism. First, there had to be an attack on the foundation upon which Western civilization and its future depended, the family unit and structure. The traditional patriarchal family structure is as old as Western Christendom 's Civilization itself. The creation of such a system perhaps predates Christianity, but it is Christianity that has taught and endorsed the idea that men were to lead the family. The Bible commands women to submit unto their husbands, for the Man is the head of the wife.[xl] The Patriarchal system meant that women were responsible for the most important job of all, raising the children. As commanded by the Bible in Genesis to be "fruitful and multiply," women were responsible for the rearing of multiple children as many as 14 or 15 children per family was considered common place only a century ago. This traditional Christian family structure was brought into question by the communist secret agent, Betty Freidman. Betty Freidman appeared to be a typical 1950's American mother. Her appeal was that she was just like all the other American women, *exploited by men*. Her argument was that for a woman to fully be independent, she had to find self-fulfillment not in her family and the raising of her kids but in a career. Betty failed to mention that during her college years at Smith College, she was a communist propagandist. Had women known that she was secretly a communist, she probably wouldn't have sold over 5 million copies of her book, *The Feminist Mystique* which effectively incited women to attack traditional fundamental Christian and Western beliefs.

 The women's movement or the second wave of feminism was a movement for the equality of women which was a "smoke screen for a diabolical crusade to destroy the heterosexual family. For example, Friedrich Engels said, "The first condition of the liberation of the wife is to bring the whole female sex back into public industry, and this in turn demands the abolition of the monogamous family as the economic unit of society."[xli] The extreme view of feminism in its current wave in the 21st century discourages and even shamefully looks down upon women of a traditional family structure. They are viewed by popular culture as backward; backward mainly because they want to raise their offspring. According to Henry Makow, "women have been psychologically neutered," encouraged to pursue sex and career not marriage and family.[xlii] This naturally effected the West in two ways. One, society thought the Biblical command of submission of a woman to her loving husband was ridiculous, peeling away at Biblical principles for a Christian society. Second, it created a situation in which the family no longer could be large. The average Western woman today has between 1.3 to 1.8 kids,[xliii] which means as a civilization, the West is shrinking. It also means that women are finding it more difficult to raise children with their demands at work and with the divorce rate at all time high in the history of Western civilization, this often means they must do it alone. So they have less kids, and the kids they do have are taught by the school system essentially everything about life, from where the world comes from to morals and ethics which is exactly what the communists want, they want to teach Western kids, to ensure the eventual demise of religion and capitalism. The Public school system hence has become responsible for the moral ethical teaching of children in the place of their parents whom are increasingly spending less time with their kids and more time at work. With parents being less involved in their 1.8 children and a shrinking population, the West was forced to adapt the open immigration act, in the United States this took place in 1968. To sustain a growing economy, the average children per family should be around 2.2. To compensate for the lack of population growth, the open immigration act brought millions of Muslim immigrants to the West. The West became a multicultural society. The idea of multiculturalism is a communist idea in itself, in that communism is opposed to nationalism. Multiculturalism naturally made many people feel xenophobic. So Western governments introduced cultural awareness programs and other initiatives to try to push people of other civilizations to assimilate to Western ideals. When these initiatives largely failed, it was the Western governments that started appeasing the immigrants and assimilating to their ideas, religion and culture. The governments of the west introduced a policy I call *the anything goes in the name of tolerance policy*. In the name of tolerance the liberal policy makers (hidden Communists) have gone on the offensive against the Christian religion in the absolute secularization of government even though many European nations have an established national church and Christianity is enshrined in their constitutions and Laws, all in the name of tolerance for other religions and for the growing number of atheists. For example, in the United States children are no longer required to pledge allegiance to the flag, since in the pledge there is the mention of God. If Lenin were alive, he would probably do a dance. In reality, other religions had not complained, it is all an atheist communist conspiracy.

Nothing is more evident to the extent of the infiltration of communist ideals in the West than the European Union charter which makes no mention of God or of its Christian heritage. The United Nations likewise, created by Western nations made no attribution to Christianity, its past or its heritage, but there is a Pagan statue at the UN of Zeus. Although the Church is not dead per say, in many European nations being a true Christian believer is that of an extreme minority. Even Pope Benedict XVI noted that the re-Christianization of Europe was the main focus of his papacy. The success of communism is best seen in the moral decline of society webbed with the rising number of atheists. The control of the Media became the best propaganda machine for the communists. Communists always had a grasp on the artists. The Media is perhaps the best mind control propaganda machine ever known to man. They control a large sector of television programs, through movies, music clips, and music in general. Frank Shaeffer calls this the "media class." The sexualization of society through Hollywood, and through our public school system. Just this year in a Wisconsin a public school, the school curriculum entailed detailed instruction to 4th graders dealing with subjects on sex, and masturbation.[xliv]

The total destruction of censorship in the West created the idolization of stars like Miley Cyrus displayed nude on television for all the young kids to see, idolize and mimic. Any idea of traditional decency or morality is considered backward and attacked as people belonging to a society of "Jesus Freaks." The abolishment of Sodomy Laws, as Justice Scalia put it, was the end of all morality laws in America which America is considered the most conservative of Western nations.

> In the absence of religiously motivated self-restraint and the mitigating communitarian influence of traditional social structures such as churches and families, all that remains as a bulwark against the nightmare of the social breakdown the expanding, apparently limitless intrusive power of the secular state. The social engineer, the doctor, the tax man, the court pierces

progressive condom dispensing schoolteacher/sex educator, the regulatory bureaucratic, ever-expanding government programs, absent family integrity, religious faith and individual responsibility, are constantly presented by our government and media knowledge class, as last best hope for maintaining social order. [xlv]

The Communist have what they wanted, an increasingly atheistic immoral society. When Christmas season is upon us, notice how most retail store employee's refuse to say Merry Christmas to consumers any longer as it has always been since Christmas was celebrated in the West, all in the name of tolerance. Where is the tolerance for Christianity then? Take not during Christmas or other Christian holidays how cable TV programs are often on subjects that cast doubt on the foundations of the Christian faith by supposed historical and scientific experts. Yet, the fundamental hatred of religion is only reflected against Christianity, but Islam is now considered a protected untouchable religion in the West and is spared from similar programs attacking the Islamic faith. The same goes for Hinduism and its philosophy and Judaism.

The mass immigration of non Westerners to the West, was a communist conspiracy brought to us by leftist communist elected leaders, which used democracy as a pawn to spread the idea of tolerance which in reality was meant to subjugate Christianity and its symbols in the public sphere. Only in Western countries do the ideals of a civilization's religion in which its laws are based upon are not allowed to be taught to their school children in the name of tolerance for non- Western immigrants children. Even though the Christian message is universal and for all peoples, not just Westerners. The West is changing, as President Obama noted in his speech in June 2007, "Whatever we once were, we are no longer a Christian nation, at least, not just. We are also a Jewish nation, a Muslim nation, a Buddhist nation, and a Hindu nation, and a nation of nonbelievers."[xlvi] ... Therefore, in the name of tolerance we teach our children common universal communist morality since we can no longer teach strictly Christian morality, since our lands are no longer Christian only societies. So they teach our children through the lens of communism. Yet so many things have gone wrong in our society, and we often question why. Frank Shaeffer said it best,

> those secularists who often shout the loudest for new programs and initiatives to combat the growing social anarchy are like stone throwing window smashers who also happens to own the only window repair shop in town. The failure of their own coercive and intrusive programs will only provide them with further evidence for the need of even more intrusion into people's lives in order to create a "new society" a "new man", a "new woman", a "new world order", a "new multicultural, gender-neutral utopia" in which everything will be tolerated except politically incorrect, "old-fashioned," "regressive" religious ideas. [xlvii]

The feminist movement which surely had some legitimate claims was taken to new levels by the hidden communist social engineers whom sought to elevate women to resemble the attributes of men, and to likewise, present to men a less former, redefined man by feminizing him. The fine line between men and women has morphed into a culture that needs books to define what makes a man a man and what makes a woman a women, because we are a generation that is confused to our gender roles; men wear earrings, women get tattoos, all the traditional boundaries have been made fuzzy. The NBA has a female referee and some men are stay at home dads, things have changed quite a bit. One of the best ways to attack religious beliefs is through feminism in which most of the religions of the world have distinct roles for women and for men. In Christianity, Judaism and Islam, there is the patriarchal system, in which the Man is the head of the family. The power given to man by God in all three religions differ, but only slightly. Communist whom are seeking to destroy Western civilization used feminism as one of their most powerful tools. Viewing religion as a backward system created by men to suit men. How much has changed? View the roles found in shows like, "All in the family," "The Honeymooners" or "I love Lucy" to "Married with

Children" or "Modern Family" and notice the difference in the roles of the characters and even what we find funny as a society which has entirely been redefined.

It seems that no single political interest group has more devoutly proclaimed the new secularized gospel of academic fundamentalism then have the feminists. No single group has pushed harder to have traditional Christian religion regulated to the inconsequential neither world of personal experience or for a harder to perpetuate the idea that traditional Jewish and Christian religious truth is "regressive" and, therefore, those do not belong in the public arena; and should not even be given a hearing. Feminist literary criticism has followed deconstructionist ideological lines by reading into all literature, past and present, a radically revisionist interpretation that superimposes an image of patriarchal tyranny and gender oppression on to all literature at the expense of most traditional interpretations or spiritual and trends and to themes once held to be common to all people, races and sexes down through the ages. [xlviii]

One big (straight, gay, multicultural, traditional) happy family

Chapter 7

The West is Evil

"The modern bourgeois society that has sprouted from the ruins of feudal society has not done away with class antagonisms. It has but established new classes, new conditions of oppression, new forms of struggle in place of the old ones."

— Karl Marx

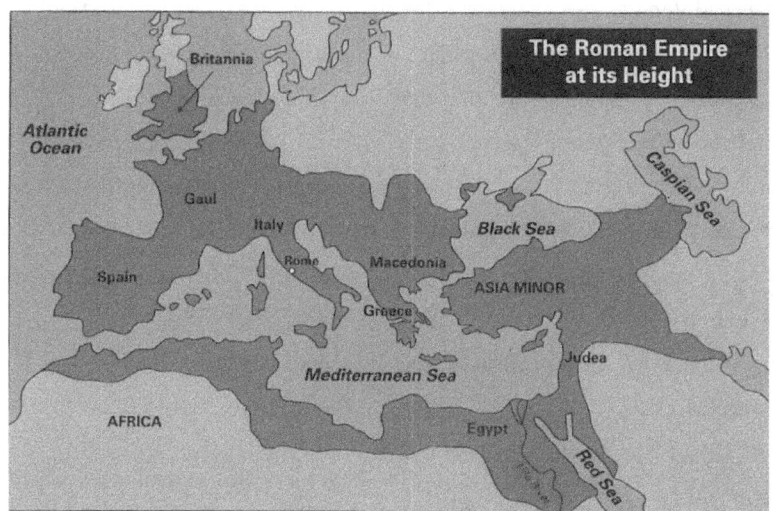

When I was an undergraduate student at Rutgers University, I studied Political Science and minored in History. I recall taking a class, "the History of Western Civilization" in which the entire curriculum was bashing of the West, as if the West had never offered anything good to the rest of humanity, which is completely false. It was as if Lenin himself was teaching my course. The entire curriculum was dedicated to the evils of the Catholic Church, Christianity, and the White Man, while proclaiming the advancements of medieval Islamic societies. The class also stressed the victimization of Muslims and the Islamic Empire at the hands of Christian Crusaders and imperialists. The dedication to the Crusades was given top priority, a good two weeks, 4 lectures in which there was never any mention of the Islamic Jihad that had invaded and subjugated parts of Christendom hundreds of years before Christians decided to go on the offensive mainly through the advent of a "crusade" by Pope Urban the II in which he urged the faithful to help save their Christian brethren whom were being slaughtered by Muslims in Palestine. As I read Pope Urban's speech, I thought of the Christians of the Middle East today, and how they are still being slaughtered for their faith, especially in Syria by the Free Syrian Army in which is made up of jihadist combatants from across the Muslim world. Yet, I couldn't help but think that at least back then when Pope Urban called on the first Crusade there still was a Christendom, but today; Christendom is no more, instead we have the secularist West. Who would come to the aid of these innocent Christians that live within Dar el Islam; after all, according to our liberal Western professors, that would be evil European imperialism.

> ... the politicizing of the study of history and literature results in a sort of cultural amnesia, a deculturization in which our secularized cultural elite seem to be bent on forcing the members of our society into forgetting who they are and where they came from as the first necessary step in engineering our society into a new secular utopia. [xlix]

Just like when the communists, as discussed earlier, took over Russia and declared the separation of church from school, their main focal point of attack was on the traditional school curriculum, likewise; the same is happening all across the West in which our universities are producing the next stage, which is the gradual evolution of our political system according to Marxism, from capitalism to socialism which will eventually lead to communism. Our historical heritage of Christendom is increasingly ignored while the glaring problems of non-Christians societies are increasingly covered up and falsely promoted. "If one reads the average history textbook used in our schools today, one would think that the 1000 years of Byzantine civilization with its art, theology, humane philanthropic institutions, commerce and literature had never existed and had nothing to do with us. Our students are urged to study Australian aborigine culture or rain forest ecology or the literary proclamations of the lesbian, African-Americans or homosexual lifestyles, while not learning about St. Constantine the great, St. John Chrysostom, Shakespeare, Dostoevsky, Chaucer, Charlotte Bronte, or Mark Twain." There is no other place on earth, no other civilization that self loathes the way Westerns do. For example, if you study history in a Muslim country, history begins with Islam in that land, ignoring pre-Islamic societies as if they never existed. For example, in Egypt and most other Arab and Islamic countries, they do not tell their students that Islam had invaded through a military campaign. They refuse to teach their students that there was an exceptional Empire named Byzantium in which Islam invaded. They don't teach that Islam forced its non-Muslim citizens to pay three times higher taxes than the taxes that were there under Byzantine rule, nor do they tell their students that Islam forced these taxes on the natives while making them feel subdued and second class to the Muslims. Unlike Western civilization that promotes self hate, in Muslim countries, and all other civilizations in the world, their public school curriculum negates any negativity associated with their nation's honor, religion, culture and society. Naturally, they have a lot of bad things to say about the West. So not only is every other civilization in the world taught to hate the West, but the West teaches their own students to hate themselves and their forefathers as well. This creates a feeling of guilt for the Westerner, a feeling of apathy towards their own civilization, it creates a feeling that western civilization is not worth fighting for, dying for, or even defending. There is no greater example of this than the Madrid 2003 train bombings, in which Islamists who had immigrated to Spain decided to terrorize the Spaniards for their support in the Iraq war. Islamic Terror works in Europe, because Europeans blame themselves for the Islamic terror, rather than looking at Islam as the true culprit in their crimes against innocent civilians. A few weeks after the Madrid bombings, the Spanish elected a Leftist government, which immediately pulled out of the Iraq war under threat and in appeasement of the Islamists. The people asked and pondered on the question of why do the Islamists hate us? Their answer will not surprise you by now which was to be dismissive; it can't be religious motivated... It must be something we can relate to, poverty, oppression, colonialism. The neo-Marxist analysis came easily, from these misreading of reality spring a host of colossally wrongheaded responses."[1] The Spaniards forgot their own history in which Muslim Jihadists invaded and occupied the southern part of Spain for over 700 years until on January 2, 1492, Emir Muhammad XII surrendered the Emirate of Granada to Queen Isabella I of Castile, and her husband King Ferdinand II of Aragon. Another good example is Dutch Politian Wilhelmus Simon Petrus Fortuijn, who authored many books and openly spoke on the dangers of Islam to Western civilization through the open immigration act.

> I am defending and protecting this country that we've built up over five, six centuries. What we now have here, God damn it, is a kind of fifth column.

People who are capable of destroying this country... I have no desire to defend their interests. That is why I tell them; you can stay here in this country, but you have to adapt... I refuse to hear repeatedly that Allah is great all mighty and powerful, and I am a dirty pig. You are a Christian dog, and an infidel. That's what they shout! And you accept this and keep silent.... You have made yourselves their doormat.

- Petrus Fortuijn

Petrus Fortuijn had had enough of the spineless, leftist leaning political order and decided to run for the highest office in the Netherlands. According to early polls he was in the lead. 9 days before election day, Volkert van der Graaf ambushed Fortuijn, dispensing six bullets into his head, neck and chest. Fortuijn died from his wounds. Ironically, the white Dutch native who killed Fortuijn was an animal rights activist who fought for the rights of animals, yet to Graff, Fortuijn was less worthy of life than an animal. When asked why he had done it, he answered saying that he found Fortuijn a danger to society because his view of Islam was "stigmatizing," and that he had murdered him to deny him political power,[li] the axis of evil at its best. The leftist leaning, secret communists who led European politics and institutions since WWII ended are to blame for the destruction of Western Civilization in the years to come. They have opened the doors to the feminist movement that caused a decrease in fertility rates of Native Westerners in which the only answer to solve the problem was to open its doors to non-Western immigrants, most troubling; Muslim immigrates of whom have been trying to invade Western Europe since the inception of Islam. Bernard Lewis, perhaps the most distinguished Western expert on Islam, predicted that Europe would be Islamic by the end of the 21st century. Anyone who doubts his assertion need only to look at the numbers and statistics in which no propagandist is needed. Today, and in most of Western Europe, the Muslim share of the population is somewhere between 2 and 20 percent. In Sweden, Austria, and the Netherlands, the figure approaches the high end of that range. In France, it's 12 percent; in Switzerland, it's an astonishing 20 percent. A glance at the relative rates of reproduction suggests that this percentage will rise perceptual story over the coming generation. Among native Western Europeans, the fertility rate ranges from 1.22 to 1.8, well below the replacement rate of 2.1. This means that the native population of Western countries will decline considerably over the next generation, and the number of retired persons will approach the number of employed persons, causing an economic crisis. Meanwhile, the number of Muslims will increase dramatically, partly through continued immigration and partly through reproduction. The fertility rate of Muslims in Europe is around 6:1. Already, in most of Western Europe, 16 to 20 percent of children are Muslims. Within a few years, every fifth or sixth young adult in Western Europe will be a Muslim; within a couple of generations, most European countries will have Muslim majorities. The Imams know this; "Muslims have a dream of living in an Islamic society," declared a Danish Muslim leader in 2000. "This dream will surely be fulfilled in Denmark... we will eventually be a majority." A T-shirt popular among young Muslims in Stockholm reads: "2030, then we take over." There are already places across Europe that have designated areas for Muslims in which secular laws need not apply. In these areas, like in East London for example, Muslim thugs roam the streets proclaiming their neighborhoods as Islamic territory. They take it into their own hands to carry out God's laws by forbidding that which God has forbidden disregarding the host countries laws.[lii] Shockingly, when the Natives try to stand up to the Muslim thugs, they are the ones arrested by the police, and the media usually labels them as xenophobic bigots. Amazingly, there are Muslim majority countries that don't obide by these strict Islamic laws.

Sign found plastered on a London street wall

Signs found in East London proclaiming Sharia Zones

Jesus and Mo

UK censorship keeps the name of Jesus, but refuses to write
Mohammad out of fear of offending British Muslims.

Infamous banner used by UK Cleric who planned a Sharia Rally in D.C.: 'Rise to Implement the Sharia campaign in America'

Concluding Thoughts

The European flag   - and our future?

Six of the seven treaties abolishing Britain as a nation have already been signed by the Queen.

What have you done to stop the march of the EU police state?

The communist infiltration was like a small virus that entered into the host, into Western Civilization. At first, there were no symptoms, a few leftist bombings here and there that the government quickly controlled. Yet the virus multiplied and spread, slowly but surely, under the radar. The ideas of communism that the Germans feared so much that they locked Lenin in his room on the train to Petrograd in 1917 in fear that his ideas would spread among the Germans, brought us the Feminist Movement, the Sexual Revolutions and the Gay Rights movement among other changes was a sign of changing times and a changing civilization. The fact that so many women and men revolted, stood up and rebelled for these changes within our civilization was a sign that the foundation of our Civilization which had been there for almost two millennium was losing its influence on Western society. Christianity and it's principles were weakening and quickly becoming forgotten. Yet the virus never came in the name of communism, and the majority of the women and men that stood up for the Feminist Revolution, the Sexual Revolution and others never thought that it would reach the point in which the traditional family dynamic is continually under threat to serve the communist agenda; the destruction of traditional family is the destruction of the very foundation of Christianity. The communists believe in all the norms of today's Western civilization. Communists believe in a genderless utopia, a raceless utopia; that is a world without nations and borders, a world without religion, a world without religious morals, a multicultural world and a classless utopia. Most of these beliefs are exclusively present in the West only, and not anywhere else. The weakening of Christianity, has brought upon us a chaotic, anarchic society that is self destructing. From mall shootings, to record numbers of divorce, Gay marriage in which even those of Ancient Greece in all there decadence never thought of. In our society they have us convinced that heterosexuals no longer want to be monogamous, yet homosexuals want to be; have we entered into the twighlight Zone? Everything has been redefined and flipped upside down at the hands of the communist secret agents. Their main objective was to attack the traditional family through many different venues, anything to keep us from procreating in large numbers. The open immigration act that brought Muslims to the West to have adequate numbers of population replacement is not the fault of Muslims, whom sought a better life for themselves and their families. Yet the Muslims of the 1960s are not like the Muslims of the 21st century. Surprisingly, Islam has had a reawakening thanks to the likes of Sayyid Qutb and other influential Islamic leaders that created a return to fundamental Muslim beliefs and practices. Most of the world that is at war today has a Muslim element involved, in one way or another. These 2nd, 3rd and 4th generation Muslims are not white, are not actually British or French or German or whatever other nation they immigrated too. Just because their passport says they are from a Western nation, does not actually make them from the West. They know this, and feel closer to the lands of their fathers in which many had never seen nor know much about. They cling together at the Mosques and form a minority ingroup, in which the Muslim leaders take hold of their young minds and convince them that the West and their host nations treat them unfairly. That the West is imperialistic and evil in its nature and that the West kills innocent Muslims overseas. All while the leftist governments across the West, cater too, and appease Islamists demands while cracking down on Western nationalists whom are labeled bigots and racists. We have unknowingly brought upon ourselves and within our midst a forgotten enemy of our civilization, in which our forefathers fought for generations since the inception of Islam in 640AD. The reality is Muslims are becoming more fundamentalist, more extreme in their interpretation of their religion, while Christianity in the West has never been weaker in its history. With Muslim families procreating 6 times as much as native Westerners, it is only a matter of time till they are a strong enough voting block to demand Islamic principles in their host state, and rightfully so, that is after all what a democracy is, isn't it? A few more years from there they will be the Majority, and they might demand the legislation of Islamic Law. With the majority, we will find in the West Muslims become presidents and prime ministers, defense ministers and parliament majority members. As this happens in some Western nations father than others, you will see a change in foreign policy and perhaps the breaking up of the EU. The possibilities are endless, but I fear that the inevitable will happen, and in our life time; a civil war across Europe. Perhaps the communists missed a calculation or two. Perhaps they predicted that by the time Muslims were the majority the entire idea of any religion would be dead anyway. I wouldn't count on it, and the Muslims don't play nice the way the Christians do, they aren't pacifists. Communists will be the first to be hunted down and slaughtered for their lack of faith per Islamic Sharia Law; atheists are to be killed.[liii] I predict that before Muslims reach the tipping point of the majority a group of conservative native Europeans will emerge across the continent, forming militia groups to counter the Islamic threat, in which a civil war will break out, between Muslims, natives and leftist government forces. This will happen as Muslims increasingly grow in numbers and in political power. When they have established a powerful enough base, they will begin to legislate through their own elected officials or through leftist leaning politicians who hope to appease Muslims. What will secular Muslims do? Psychologically, most minorities stick to an ingroup so that they can be protected. Those secular Muslims will try to free themselves from the Islamists, but in the end they might have to side with them; at least in a total all out European Civil War the Islamists would kill them as traitors and the Natives would view them as Islamist enemies; just by the way they look like the Sikhs that were murdered after 911 by illiterate Neanderthal that thought they were Muslim. by then, there will be total anarchy and many secular Muslims I believe might leave the West for safety in their home countries or the countries of their fathers. After which Turkey might join the war and aid the Muslims. Will the U.S. stand and watch and declare the civil war a European problem like in the beginnings of WWI and WWII? There are many unknowns, but we can only make predictions according to current trends, however; if the trends change sooner than later the dim outcome may be avoided. Much of the responsibility of the fate of the West lies on Christianity and its established churches. A reawakening Church and its institutions could persuade voters to vote for conservatives in which the Muslim problem in the West could be dealt with before Muslims reach the 35% mark. Christianity must retain itself in the European consciousness. If the Church remains a museum, and the schools and society continues in its communist leftist path, I am afraid Western Civilization will not fight for itself until Muslims form a majority and begin to implement Sharia Law and native Europeans then will suffer the same fate as their brethren had in the Middle Eastern/ North African region of the Byzantine Empire centuries ago. Just because we want to preserve our heritage and civilization that does not make us bigots or racists. Only in the West do we allow people of other civilizations that are from different religions and cultures become citizens of our lands, effectively changing the landscape of the West openly and willingly. Anyone against such policy is labeled by the communists as xenophobic and intolerant. Yet, the entire world must be xenophobic since all Muslim countries in which one can immigrate to refuse to give non-natives citizenship. If an Indian Christian wanted to work in the Bahrain for example, they apply for a workers visa. They can live and work in the Bahrain freely, and when their time is up, they must return to where they came from. And this non citizenship type of policy is not just restricted to the Muslim world, all other nations that are not Western also follow these same policies like Japan and other Asian nations. The West needs to reform immigration by restricting non-Westerners from applying for citizenship. Those who enter the West should have Western ideals like Arab Christians for example.

The United States leads the West and is exceptional. The United States is the only Western power that still has the guts to fight. Still has the military capability to bring the war to the enemy. The United States carries the torch of Western Civilization. In the United States we have seen the communists at work for some time, we tend to be behind Europe some 15 years or so. I hope for America's sake, and for all of Western Civilization's sake, that conservatives take over after President Obama finishes his last term in office. President Obama was the long awaited dream or savior for leftist leaning communists. We all know that communists have infiltrated the white house for some time now, but no President has pushed us more towards socialism and communism than President Obama. No one has hurt Western Civilization more than President Obama. Tomorrows battlefield will be on European soil, let us hope that the U.S. will be prepared to intervene and play a major role in aiding and defending our fellow Westerners during the civil war in which the fate of the West will be on the line. Which side the U.S. supports depends heavily on whether the current trends remain the same, or whether changes occur in the leftist communist trend before we reach that apocalyptic predicted civil war; only time will solve this mystery.

All that is necessary for the triumph of evil is that good men do nothing.

-Edmund Burke

Quotes to Consider:

Within the philosophical system of Marx and Lenin, and at the heart of their psychology, hatred of God is their principal driving force, more fundamental than all their political and economic pretensions. Militant atheism is not merely incidental or marginal to Communist policy. It is not a side effect, but the central pivot. -Alexander Solzhenitsyn

Morality is that which serves to destroy the old exploiting society.... We deny all morality that is drawn from some conception beyond men, beyond class. We say that it is a deception, ... a fraud and a stultification of the minds of the workers and peasants in the interests of the landowners and capitalists.

-Lenin

"أُمِرْتُ أَنْ أُقاتِلَ النَّاسَ حَتَّى يَشْهَدُوا أَنْ لاَ إِلَهَ إِلاَّ اللهُ وَأَنَّ مُحَمَّدًا رَسُولُ اللهِ، وَيُقِيمُوا الصَّلاَةَ، وَيُؤْتُوا الزَّكَاةَ؛ فَإِذَا فَعَلُوا ذَلِكَ عَصَمُوا مِنِّي دِمَاءَهُمْ وَأَمْوَالَهُمْ إِلاَّ بِحَقِّ الإِسْلاَمِ، وَحِسَابُهُمْ عَلَى اللهِ تَعَالَى" .

رَوَاهُ الْبُخَارِيُّ [رقم:25]، وَمُسْلِمٌ [رقم:22]

I have been ordered to laughter the people until they testify that there is none worthy of worship except Allah and that Muhammad is the Messenger of Allah, and until they establish the salah and pay the zakat. And if they do that then they will have gained protection from me for their lives and property, unless [they commit acts that are punishable] in Islam, and their reckoning will be with Allah.

- al-Bukhari and Muslim

Although, O sons of God, you have promised more firmly than ever to keep the peace among yourselves and to preserve the rights of the church, there remains still an important work for you to do. Freshly quickened by the divine correction, you must apply the strength of your righteousness to another matter which concerns you as well as God. For your brethren who live in the east are in urgent need of your help, and you must hasten to give them the aid which has often been promised them. For, as the most of you have heard, the Turks and Arabs have attacked them and have conquered the territory of Romania [the Greek empire] as far west as the shore of the Mediterranean and the Hellespont, which is called the Arm of St. George. They have occupied more and more of the lands of those Christians, and have overcome them in seven battles. They have killed and captured many, and have destroyed the churches and devastated the empire. If you permit them to continue thus for awhile with impurity, the faithful of God will be much more widely attacked by them. On this account I, or rather the Lord, beseech you as Christ's heralds to publish this everywhere and to persuade all people of whatever rank, foot-soldiers and knights, poor and rich, to carry aid promptly to those Christians and to destroy that vile race from the lands of our friends. I say this to those who are present, it meant also for those who are absent. Moreover, Christ commands it. "All who die by the way, whether by land or by sea, or in battle against the pagans, shall have immediate remission of sins. This I grant them through the power of God with which I am invested. O what a disgrace if such a despised and base race, which worships demons, should conquer a people which has the faith of omnipotent God and is made glorious with the name of Christ! With what reproaches will the Lord overwhelm us if you do not aid those who, with us, profess the Christian religion! Let those who have been accustomed unjustly to wage private warfare against the faithful now go against the infidels and end with victory this war which should have been begun long ago. Let those who for a long time, have been robbers, now become knights. Let those who have been fighting against their brothers and relatives now fight in a proper way against the barbarians. Let those who have been serving as mercenaries for small pay now obtain the eternal reward. Let those who have been wearing themselves out in both body and soul now work for a double honor. Behold! on this side will be the sorrowful and poor, on that, the rich; on this side, the enemies of the Lord, on that, his friends. Let those who go not put off the journey, but rent their lands and collect money for their expenses; and as soon as winter is over and spring comes, let him eagerly set out on the way with God as their guide.

-Pope Urban II - Speech to insight the first Crusade

Bibliography

AN-NAWAWĪ'S FORTY HADITH : AN ANTHOLOGY OF THE SAYINGS OF THE PROPHET MUHAMMAD. Cambridge, UK: Islamic Texts Society, 1997

Bawer, Bruce. WHILE EUROPE SLEPT : HOW RADICAL ISLAM IS DESTROYING THE WEST FROM WITHIN. New York: Doubleday, 2006

Colley, Rupert. *The Russian Revolution: History in an Hour*. HarperCollins Publishers.

Courtois, Stéphane, and Mark Kramer. THE BLACK BOOK OF COMMUNISM : CRIMES, TERROR, REPRESSION. Cambridge, Mass. London, England: Harvard University Press, 1999

Figes, Orlando. A PEOPLE'S TRAGEDY : A HISTORY OF THE RUSSIAN REVOLUTION. New York, NY: Viking, 1997

Gabel, Paul. *And God Created Lenin: Marxism vs Religion In Russia, 1917-1929*. Kindle Edition

Lenin, V. I., *Religion*. Kindle Edition
Makow, Henry. *Cruel Hoax - Feminism & New World Order*. Silas Green
Marx, Karl & Friedrich Engels. *The Communist Manifesto*

Marx, Karl & Friedrich Engels. The *Origins of the Family, Private Property and the State* (New York, International Publishers, 1942

Naqīb, Aḥmad, and Noah H. Keller. RELIANCE OF THE TRAVELER : THE CLASSIC MANUAL OF ISLAMIC SACRED LAW 'UMDAT AL-SALIK. Beltsville, MD, U.S.A: Amana Publications, 1999

Quṭb, Sayyid. SOCIAL JUSTICE IN ISLAM. Oneonta, N.Y: Islamic Publications International, 2000

Schaeffer, Frank. Dancing alone : *the quest for Orthodox faith in the age of false religion*. Brookline, Mass: Holy Cross Orthodox Press, 1994

Schmidt, Alvin J., *How Christianity Changed the World*. Kindle Edition

Endnotes

[1] Kill those who do not have faith in Allah nor [believe] in the Last Day, nor forbid what Allah and His Apostle have forbidden, nor practice the true religion (Islam), even from among those who are the people of the Book(Christians & Jews), until they pay the Jizya (tribute) out of hand, feeling subdued & degraded. (Quran, Surat al Tawba 9:29)

قَاتِلُوا الَّذِينَ لَا يُؤْمِنُونَ بِاللَّهِ وَلَا بِالْيَوْمِ الْآخِرِ وَلَا يُحَرِّمُونَ مَا حَرَّمَ اللَّهُ وَرَسُولُهُ وَلَا يَدِينُونَ دِينَ الْحَقِّ مِنَ

الَّذِينَ أُوتُوا الْكِتَابَ حَتَّىٰ يُعْطُوا الْجِزْيَةَ عَنْ يَدٍ وَهُمْ صَاغِرُونَ(Quran; Surat al Tawba 9:29)

[2] http://www.pewresearch.org/fact-tank/2014/01/08/what-is-appropriate-attire-for-women-in-muslim-countries/

[3] Islamist indoctrinating Syrian Children
http://www.youtube.com/watch?v=ExA0xQEYlMY

---

[i] Schmidt, Alvin J., *How Christianity Changed the World.* Kindle Edition, Location 165

[ii] Lenin, V. I., *Religion.* Kindle Edition, Kindle Locations 139-143

[iii] Quran, Surat al Tawba 9:29

[iv] Pope Urban II Crusading Speech 1095

[v] Special Eurobarometer, biotechnology, page 381" Fieldwork: Jan-Feb 2010

[vi] Pope expresses hope that Catholic, Orthodox re-evangelize Europe.
http://www.catholicnews.com/data/stories/cns/0602562.htm

[vii] Gabel, Paul. *And God Created Lenin: Marxism vs Religion In Russia, 1917-1929.* Kindle Edition, Kindle Locations 172-174

[viii] Lenin, 139-142

[ix] Gabel, 542

[x] Gabel, 550-553

[xi] Gabel, 1068-1073

[xii] Gabel, 1091-1093

[xiii] Colley, Rupert. *The Russian Revolution: History in an Hour*. Harper Collins Publishers. Kindle Locations 108-115

[xiv] Colley, 221-231

[xv] Colley, 430-436

[xvi] Gabel, 1749-1751

[xvii] Gabel, 1744-1745

[xviii] Gabel, 1754-1756

[xix] Ibid, 1758-1706

[xx] Bukharin in The ABC of Communism, 1922

[xxi] Bukharin in The ABC of Communism, 1922

[xxii] Colley, 460-467

[xxiii] Courtois, Stéphane, and Mark Kramer. *The Black Book of Communism: Crimes, Terror, Repression.*Cambridge, Mass. London, England: Harvard University Press, 1999, 77

[xxiv] Courtois & Kramer, 74

[xxv] Figes, Orlando. *A People's Tragedy. A History of The Russian Revolution*. New York, NY: Viking, 1997, 535

[xxvi] Figs, 535

[xxvii] Courtois & Kramer, 78

[xxviii] Gabel, 1850-1858

[xxix] Colley, 565-567

[xxx] Naqīb, Aḥmad, and Noah H. Keller. *Reliance of the Traveler: The Classic Manual of Islamic Sacred Law*. Umdat Al-Salik. Beltsville, MD, U.S.A: Amana Publications, 1999

[xxxi] The Communist Manifesto

[xxxii] Quṭb, Sayyid. *Social Justice in Islam*. Oneonta, N.Y: Islamic Publications International, 2000, 43

[xxxiii] Qutb, 45

[xxxiv] Qutb, 41

[xxxv] Qutb, 25

[xxxvi] Qutb, 47

[xxxvii] Nawawī. *An-Nawawis Forty Hadith: An Anthology of the Sayings of the Prophet Muhammad*. Cambridge, UK: Islamic Texts Society, 1997. 8th Hadith

[xxxviii] Jonathan Kwitny's Man of the Century

[xxxix] The Communist Manifesto, 20

[xl] The Holy Bible: Ephesians 5:22-23

[xli] The Origins of the Family, Private Property and the State (New York, International Publishers, 1942 p.67

[xlii] Makow, Henry. *Cruel Hoax - Feminism & New World Order*. Silas Green, 30

[xliii] Bawer, Bruce. *While Europe Slept: How Radical Islam is Destroying the West from Within.*. New York: Doubleday, 2006., 32

xliv Fox News: Wisconsin school teaches masturbation.

http://www.foxnews.com/us/2013/08/23/some-wis-schools-to-teach-masturbation-to-fourth-graders/

xlv Schaeffer, Frank. *Dancing Alone : The quest for Orthodox faith in the age of False religion.* Brookline, Mass: Holy Cross Orthodox Press, 1994.32

xlvi https://www.youtube.com/watch?v=tmC3IevZiik

xlvii Shaffer, 32

xlviii Shaffer, 22

xlix Shaffer, 24

l Bawer, 160

li Bawer, 32

lii Bawer, 32

liii Quran, 5:9